CONU
AS A NEW PET

ANMARIE BARRIE

CONTENTS

Photos by: Dr. Herbert R. Axelrod, David Alderton, Thomas Brosset, Isabelle Francais, Fred Harris, Dieter Hoppe, Horst Mayer, Horst Muller, Robert Pearcy, Chris Rowley, Harald Schultz, Vogelpark Walsrode, Michael Warren. Illustrations: John Quinn

© Copyright 1994 by T.F.H. Publications, Inc.

Distributed in the UNITED STATES to the Pet Trade by T.F.H. Publications, Inc., One T.F.H. Plaza, Neptune City, NJ 07753; distributed in the UNITED STATES to the Bookstore and Library Trade by National Book Network, Inc. 4720 Boston Way, Lanham MD 20706; in CANADA to the Pet Trade by H & L Pet Supplies Inc., 27 Kingston Crescent, Kitchener, Ontario N2B 2T6; Rolf C. Hagen Ltd., 3225 Sartelon Street, Montreal 382 Quebec; in CANADA to the Book Trade by Macmillan of Canada (A Division of Canada Publishing Corporation), 164 Commander Boulevard, Agincourt, Ontario M1S 3C7; in the United Kingdom by T.F.H. Publications, PO Box 15, Waterlooville PO7 6BQ; in AUSTRALIA AND THE SOUTH PACIFIC by T.F.H. (Australia), Pty. Ltd., Box 149, Brookvale 2100 N.S.W., Australia; in NEW ZEALAND by Brooklands Aquarium Ltd. 5 McGiven Drive, New Plymouth, RD1 New Zealand; in Japan by T.F.H. Publications, Japan—Jiro Tsuda, 10-12-3 Ohjidai, Sakura, Chiba 285, Japan; in SOUTH AFRICA by Multipet Pty. Ltd., P.O. Box 35347, Northway. 4065, South Africa. Published by T.F.H. Publications, Inc.

Manufactured in the United States of America by T.F.H. Publications, Inc.

Introduction

The term "conure" was originally applied to the birds of the genus *Conures*, now renamed *Aratinga*. Today the name is used to cover a much wider group of birds. All conures are found in the neotropics of South America. They may be considered as the New World equivalents to the parakeets of Africa, Asia and Australia. They are long-tailed parrots often described as being like miniature macaws. This is true only of certain species.

In past years, conures have not proven to be especially popular birds; the situation has changed in more recent times. Today certain species are greatly sought-after. They command very high prices. The majority of species, though, remains relatively inexpensive when compared with other parrots of similar size.

Conures have two drawbacks which have restricted their popularity over the years. Firstly, most —

though by no means all— tend to be rather noisy. Secondly, they need comparatively sturdy accommodations. Conures have strong beaks which quickly destroy any unprotected wood in aviaries built for them. On their credit side, they are reasonably priced, long-lived, hardy, and many are reliable breeders. They also make superb pets if acquired at a very young age. Ideally, those which

The Jandaya Conure, *Aratinga jandaya*, is probably the most available species in the conure family.

Nanday Conure, *Nandayus nenday.* Most conures give their owners a great deal of pleasure. They have very playful and affectionate personalities, and they truly prove to be life-long companions.

have been hand-reared are the best.

Many countries are now restricting, if not totally banning, the export of their native wildlife. This has added a new interest to species which were formerly freely available. More enthusiasts are now trying to establish captive breeding programs in many parrot species, including conures.

The growing interest in this group of birds can be clearly illustrated. Over the last 15 years, the price of various species has increased considerably. For example, the popular Nanday Conure could be purchased during the early 1970s for less than £4.50 ($7). Today the same species costs at least ten times more. Patagonian Conures were selling at just £30 per pair during 1971. By 1987 they were priced at £225 ($400) in the UK. Such increases still might not be as high as for some parrot species. Conures have become much more desirable birds, a trend that is likely to continue—thus making breeding them worthwhile.

Although somewhat raucous at times, remember that many other popular parrots (such as cockatoos and amazons) can be every bit as disruptive. Conures

conures do. Availability of conures is restricted to a few species. Thus they may be considered more of a specialist's choice if required for breeding. This fact is a definite plus in their favor. If you plan to breed, the price need not be cut in order to sell your birds. This is often the case with other Australian species.

It is not possible, within the limitations of this book, to discuss every existing conure species. Most of those likely to be available are listed. Included is practical information on how to choose, accommodate, feed, breed and generally care for your birds. The idea is to obtain the maximum pleasure from them, whether kept in an aviary or in your home as a family pet.

have possibly been unfairly singled out in this aspect. A number of conure species can be considered very quiet when compared to cockatoos or macaws.

As a group, conures do not exhibit the flamboyant colors of the Australian parakeets, however, few Australian parakeets make suitable pets whereas most

Natural History

NOMENCLATURE

It is very useful that the newcomer to birds be familiar with the way in which they are scientifically named. This is because most magazines, books and dealers' lists use a bird's scientific name as well as its common name. The scientific name, in Latin, is internationally standard. The common name changes, not only within the country or language, but even among breeders. This can create confusion as to which species is, in fact, being discussed.

A conure is a member of the larger order of birds known as Psittaciformes— the parrots and parrot-like birds. Members of this order typically have hooked beaks. They also have two forward and two backward pointing toes to their feet. This is referred to as being zygodactyl.

Most parrots have relatively colorful plumage, though this may be restricted to the head. The remainder of the body is usually various shades of green. The Australian parakeets and certain macaws are notably gaudy exceptions to this.

Parrots are distributed throughout the world in the warmer climates. Their presence lessens in numbers as the climate gets cooler. They are totally absent in Europe, North America and the polar regions.

The order Psittaciformes is

The Golden-capped Conure, *Aratinga auricapilla,* is becoming a highly popular species. It grows to a length of 30 cm (12in), and the orange-red on the forehead and chest is set off by its green body plumage and its black beak and feet.

divided into three families: the cockatoos (Cacatuidae), the lories (Loriidae) and the true parrots (Psittacidae). The conures belong to this last group. The parrot family is further divided into many groups known as genera (singular genus). Each group contains parrots which are very similar to one another, yet they are still sufficiently different to be further subdivided into yet smaller groups, termed species. At this level the birds form interbreeding populations which remain distinct from other species of the same genus.

Even within a species there may be groups of birds that have formed isolated populations. Such populations show very small differences in their plumage and feeding habits. These birds are called subspecies. They may be regarded as examples of evolution in progress.

A species is identified as such when both the generic name and the specific name are used together. For example, the parrot known as the Sun Conure has the scientific name of *Aratinga solstitialis.* There are many other conures in the genus *Aratinga,* so only by adding the second name is a particular species identified.

Within a species there may be numerous subspecies. These are identified by the specific name being repeated in the case of the first of that species to be named. After that, the other subspecies are given their own subspecific names. The original binomial name thus becomes a trinomial when discussing subspecies. An example is the Olive-throated Conure, *Aratinga nana;* this tells the species. If you wish to be even more specific then consider *Aratinga nana nana,* the Jamaican subspecies, or *Aratinga nana astec,* the Mexican subspecies. In this case, the former species, being the first named, is known as the nominate race. Repetition of the specific name automatically reveals that it was the first of that species to be recognized and named.

It is customary to write scientific names in italic. (If the text is in italics, then roman type is used.) Note that the generic name is capitalized, while the specific, or trivial name, begins in lower case.

Often a name appears after the specific name in detailed texts. This is the

Finsch's Conure, *Aratinga finschi,* originates in Nicaragua, Costa Rica and Panama but is not readily available to the bird fancier.

person who first described and named the species. Sometimes a date follows such a name. If the person's name is in parentheses, this indicates that the bird was originally placed into a different genus than the present one.

This system of nomenclature is called the binomial system. It was devised by a Swedish naturalist named Carolus Linnaeus. (He is also known as von Linnaeus or Linne.) The system was formulated during the 18th century. It has been updated many times with additional knowledge of the birds. This is why, in order to incorporate the latest thoughts on their believed relationships to one another, some species are moved from one genus to another.

Unlike common bird language, which is very general in application, scientific nomenclature is exact at any one point in time. For example, in aviculture, terms such as finches, softbills or seedeaters are very loose terms. They encompass birds which may have no real relationship with each other. Whereas, citing Psittacidae immediately restricts the birds covered to members of the parrot family.

Likewise, if you are interested in only the conures of the genus *Aratinga*, this is quite precise. It tells other breeders that your range of interest is restricted to the species that make up this particular genus. The further up the binomial system you go the more general the relationships are between the members. The lower you go, the closer you move toward the individual birds.

In their natural habitat the Patagonian Conure, *Cyanoliseus patagonus*, will excavate a suitable nesting site in sandstone cliffs. Members of this species are also known as "Burrowing Parrots."

DISTRIBUTION

Conures are found from Mexico south to Tierra del Fuego. This southernmost tip of South America is the most southerly habitat of any parrot species. conures also range across the islands of the Caribbean. In some cases, such as that of the Blue-crowned Conure, *Aratinga acuticaudata,* the area of distribution is very extensive. In other cases, as in the Rose-crowned Conure, *Pyrrhura rhodocephala*, it is extremely limited. Where the distribution is limited, any changes in the habitat, such as deforestation, can have far-reaching effects. This is seen in the case of the Golden or Queen of Bavaria Conure. It is now listed as an endangered species due to such changes.

HABITAT

Considering such an enormous range of distribution, conures are found in every possible ecological niche. Some inhabit the open grasslands, others in areas which are lightly wooded and still others live in dense tropical rainforest. Some species stay close to water courses

Olive-throated Conure, *Aratinga nana.* In the wild, this species often damages local corn crops.

at low altitude. Others are found at greater heights on mountain ranges.

The question of altitude is thus of some interest to aviculturists. Clearly there is a wide temperature fluctuation between day and night at different altitudes. Alternatively, temperature in the dense rainforest is more even and the humidity is greater. These factors affect both the overall hardiness of a species and its breeding potential. Humidity is known to be important during the incubation of eggs. However, it is a subject which aviculturists are beginning to understand only now. Knowledge of it is very sparse at this time.

SIZE

Conures range in size from 23cm (9in) to 51cm (30in). Some species, such as the Patagonian Conure, *Cyanoliseus patagonus,* are actually larger than the small macaws, though less substantially built. The smaller species are generally the more popular.

CONSERVATION AND AVICULTURE

There is a growing awareness that many animal species are now under threat of extinction. Measures must be taken to protect the birds—or more importantly, their habitats. In modern times, at least one conure species, the Carolina Conure or Parakeet, has vanished from its homelands in the U.S.A. Its extinction was a result of its persecution by man, coupled with lack of interest in its breeding in captivity. Many more species are barely coping. The extra pressures placed on them include habitual trapping, deforestation and extermination in order to protect crops upon which the birds feed. It is a problematic area in which the vested interests of many people are often in direct opposition. Some countries, such as Brazil and Chile, have taken measures to protect species or ban their export.

Others pay lip service to conservation but are unable to control habitat destruction—especially devastation resulting from mining and logging.

All of these facts strongly suggest that it is vital that birdkeepers make some attempt to breed conures.

There is a further benefit from homebred stock in that these birds are healthier, hardier and adjust more easily to a domestic environment (a home or aviary). Most Australian parrots have become well established outside their continent since export bans were placed on all fauna in 1959. The increased prices that resulted provided the impetus to establish breeding colonies.

Conures are rapidly becoming comparably bred and kept. This should provide the financial incentive for aviculturists to establish strains of the lesser seen species while they are still available.

Life in the Wild

Conures, like most other birds, are gregarious creatures. They enjoy the company of their own kind. The birds form small flocks which vary from a few pairs to those numbering hundreds. Vast flocks assemble at communal feeding areas. After feeding, they disperse to their respective roosting areas. Some species travel large distances in order to feed. Others, especially those from the dense rainforests, have little need to travel far to find sufficient food or water.

Unlike Australian parakeets, conures are very cosmopolitan in their diets. Apart from seeding grasses and leaf buds, they will consume large quantities of fruit. During the breeding period, they dramatically increase their intake of animal protein. This includes items such as invertebrates and even carrion. The pair bonds formed during the breeding season are thought to last the lifetime of the individuals.

Man is but one hazard with which the birds of the

Finsch's Conure, *Aratinga finschi*. Unfortunately, conures in the wild are suffering from the destruction of their natural habitats. Captive breeding programs must be established to propagate the species.

Cuban Conure, *Aratinga euops*, Cactus Conure, *Aratinga cactorum*, and Petz's Conure, *Aratinga canicularis*.

wild must contend. Parrots are preyed upon by most wild cat species. Snakes, hawks, owls and eagles are other predators. Other species of parrots compete for both food and suitable nesting sites.

Yet another hazard to the survival of conures is weather. For example, sudden tropical storms flood nests. Trees are often brought down in the flash floods that follow. Thus nests are destroyed and chicks lost. Likewise, forest fires, as well as hot ash from volcanoes, burn many trees and nesting sites. It can be appreciated that few conures—or indeed any animal—ever dies from old age. If not caught by a predator it is likely that an animal will die from a disease, disability or injury

that prevents it from feeding properly.

It is difficult to gauge the life expectancy of conures in the wild. No long-term banding and catching policies have been applied to them or any parrots outside of Australia. Australian parrots have been banded and later re-caught after eight or more years. Remember that they will live for further periods after being released again. Therefore, the banding accounts for only a part of the bird's known life span. It is reasonable to assume that if conures survive their first year, they may attain ten or more years in the wild. They live considerably longer in captivity because they are protected from dangers and given regular and nutritious foods.

Selecting Stock

A number of financial and practical considerations must be made after deciding to purchase a conure. Of course, accommodations are an important aspect. This need should be prepared before the bird is brought home. Other considerations are likely to include:

1. Choosing a species.
2. The cost.
3. Purpose: pet or breeding.
4. Place of purchase.
5. Questions of health.

Captive bred babies: Green-cheeked Conure, *Pyrrhura molinae,* Peach-fronted Conure, *Aratinga aurea,* Sun Conure, *Aratinga solstitialis,* and Rose-ringed Parakeet, *Psittacula krameri.*

CHOOSING A SPECIES

Green-cheeked
Conure, *Pyrrhura
molinae*.
Generally,
members of the
genus *Aratinga*
are inclined to be
more noisy and
destructive than
those of the genus
Pyrrhura. The fact
is that all conure
species can be
criticized for their
loud, screeching
voices and the
rapidity with which
they will reduce
any timberwork to
mere matchwood.

This book contains many fine full-color photographs of popular conure species which will give you a good idea of which ones appeal to you. Additional information indicates how difficult it is to acquire the species. In such a case, you may have to wait quite some time before locating the desired subject.

THE COST

The price of one or a pair of conures varies quite considerably. A number of factors contribute to this fact. Regularly imported or bred species are the least expensive since they are readily available in the greatest numbers. Imported birds are cheaper than homebred stock, however, they need more care in their early days. They are not as used to humans as homebred birds are. In most cases, domestic birds also have better plumage. The homebred bird is usually the better purchase. Some species, though, are not readily available. An imported bird may be the only realistic option.

The age of the bird affects the price. A hand-reared chick will command a higher price than an older, imported bird of unknown age. After a conure goes through its first full molt, at under one year of age, it is difficult to determine the bird's age unless a closed, year coded, metal band exists on the bird's leg. Thus, where the age is known for sure, the price is usually higher.

Sexed birds are always more expensive than those which are unsexed. Conures of both sexes are similar in appearance. This makes the purchase of true pairs difficult. It is worth the extra cost to purchase birds which are guaranteed a proven sex. Surgical sexing, called endoscopy, involves a veterinarian inserting a probe into the flanks of the birds. Through this, the vet is able to examine the internal organs, including those of sex. Alternatively, a breeder may have already bred two conures, thus they are a proven pair. Other sexing techniques are available, such as microscopy of cells to establish sex via the chromosomes. These techniques are not yet in regular use due to their high costs.

Hand-tame birds are normally more expensive than those which are not tame. Extra fees for such birds are worthwhile as this could save a great deal of time. These birds may have been tamed by the seller specifically for suitability as pets, or they may have been pet birds sold by their owners for one of many reasons. A degree of caution is needed when purchasing birds which have been previously owned; the reason may be that the conure is exceptionally

The Monk Parakeet, *Myiopsitta monachus*, is a small member of the conure family. Do not allow their small size to fool you; they still have very raucous voices.

noisy, aggressive or destructive.

The rarer conures are obviously expensive. This reflects just how difficult they are to acquire. A Queen of Bavaria Conure, *Aratinga guarouba*, is a true avian jewel. It fetches very high prices. Even a species such as Petz's Conure, *Aratinga canicularis*, very popular in the U.S.A., is still quite costly. The days of inexpensive conures seem to be a thing of the past.

The potential price permutations are innumerable. Therefore, it is not just a case of purchasing the first conure that you see of the right species. The same care should be taken when purchasing conures as you would with anything of value.

PURPOSE—PET OR BREEDING BIRDS

The purpose for which the birds are being acquired needs consideration. If the conure is to be a pet, purchase one as young as possible. A hand-reared bird is easily the favorite choice as a pet. Such a bird has no fear of humans. It will settle into your home like a new baby. The next best choice is a young bird only recently fledged. Such a bird will be steady. It quickly tames if handled gently and given much attention. The third choice is a young bird that has not yet molted; it is under one year old. A bird through its first molt is in full plumage; its age cannot be verified. Such a bird can

In the USA, the Peach-fronted conure, *Aratinga aurea,* has never been as commonly available as the Halfmoon Conure, although the situation is reversed as far as European enthusiasts are concerned.

become quite tame, however, it is not likely to attain the tameness of a young bird. Some may never tame at all, though it would be rare to find a conure that could not become hand-tame.

If you wish to purchase birds for breeding, the best choice is to purchase a proven pair of conures. That is to say, a pair which has already bred together. They are known to be compatible. The next best choice is a sexed pair advertised as S/S (surgically sexed). Here is a true pair. It is hoped they will prove compatible, of which there is more than a 50/50 chance.

PLACE OF PURCHASE

The most important consideration when deciding where to purchase your conures is the reputation of the seller. However, depending on the species sought, you may not have a great deal of choice. Pet shops are usually the best choice because they are clean, well stocked and staffed with knowledgeable sales people.

Your local pet shop dealer can also order the species of bird you specify. They will check out the bird for you; the stock should be guaranteed. A good pet shop will make sure that you are

Thick-billed Parrot, *Rhynchopsitta pachyrhyncha*. Members of this genus are said to fall between the conures and macaws in taxonomy.

fully satisfied. It is from here that you will purchase the necessary supplies and seek ongoing advice.

All birds imported into the U.S.A., the U.K. and many continental European countries have undergone a quarantine period (usually about 35 days). Therefore, you can be assured that they are feeding properly and have successfully survived the arduous weeks preceding their arrival. The plumage, however, of these birds may still appear rather unkempt. It may be soiled, or feathers may be missing or clipped. The birds will look differently after they go through a molt. Since the novice is hardly able to judge a freshly imported bird from a poor specimen, the counsel of an experienced birdkeeper is a useful resource.

A visit to a bird show with classes for parrots is strongly recommended. This way you can see what healthy conures look like. Likewise, the various parrot societies issue newsletters and monthly journals which describe and display various species. Visiting local parrot club meetings is also worthwhile. You will be made very welcome and given much worthwhile advice.

Do not rush into purchasing a conure. Take it a step at a time. See as many conures and sellers as possible. In this way, maximum satisfaction can be attained.

HEALTH

Observe a bird at a distance. This is so it is not startled into action just because you have approached its cage. An ill bird may still have sufficient energy to move around if it is nervous. Be wary of a bird that sits in the same position for a long period of time. Slowly approach the cage. If the bird still shows no interest in you, then it should be shunned.

A sleeping bird rests with one leg tucked under its feathers (an ill bird rests on two feet). Its head will be twisted 30 degrees to rest in the nape of its neck. The feathers will be fluffed up. At your approach, even the most relaxed bird should open its eye to watch you.

The eye is a vital guide to health. It should be round, clear and bright. No sign of a discharge should be present around the eyes or nostrils. Neither the cere (the fleshy part above the beak) nor the nostrils should be swollen to one side. The beak should be well formed, not overlong or poorly aligned. A few missing feathers are not generally a problem. However, bald patches indicate trouble.

A good bird has feathers in good condition. They lay tight against the body and have a shimmer about them. The feet are well formed. All four toes should be present on each foot. A missing toe will not unduly bother a pet bird, but a conure required for breeding or exhibition should be fully equipped. The scales of the legs should lay flat and not be raised. The vent region should be clear of stains or congealed feces.

Examine the droppings in the cage. They should not be hard, unduly viscous or show any signs of blood. Finally, have the bird move about its cage. It should use its beak and feet without any sign of restrictive movement. If the dealer will let you hold the conure, then by all means do so. The chest should feel firm and plump, not bony. The bird probably will flap its wings; this gives you a chance to see that they are in fine order.

The Red-masked Conure, *Aratinga erythrogenys.* The adults of this species bear a larger amount of coloring on the head than any other member of the group.

Accommodations

Conures can be safely housed in many forms of accommodation, ranging from large outdoor aviaries and indoor flights, to large cages for single pet birds. Each will be discussed, as well as useful auxiliary equipment.

OUTDOOR AVIARIES

Visit a number of breeders before actually preparing your own birds' accommodation. There is a tremendous variety of structures used for housing conures. Some are well planned, sturdily built and encompass the latest ideas in avicultural thinking. Others are interesting in that you wonder how they manage to stand up year after year. Between the two extremes, there is a vast scope of possibilities. Plan your aviaries to fit your available space, budget and number of birds to be housed.

There is little relationship between the quality of an aviary and the conures' ability to breed. Many breeders have produced healthy chicks from housing which is far from impressive. Others, with excellent facilities, have failed to

Conure aviaries in the animal park in Bretten (Germany). The dividing walls are made of chip board.

encourage birds to go to nest. Simply having the best designed aviaries by no means ensures success. This is based on many other factors. The advantages of having a well organized aviary are that routine jobs become more convenient, unwanted vermin are less able to eat the birds' food, and the birds are less likely to escape. Finally, a well-planned aviary should be an added attraction to your yard or garden. Here is where you can rest and enjoy watching your birds.

PLANNING

Plan your aviary in advance rather than haphazardly assembling a box-like structure. Impromptu structures invariably end up less than desirable. Intentions to improve this or that rarely become reality once the birds are installed.

Calculate the lengths of wood needed and the cost of the welded wire. The plans at this stage should fit your budget. A sound aviary base is also needed. Additionally, you may decide to have a walk in birdroom at the end of the flight. This is standard in the more northerly states of the U.S.A. and most of Europe. It is certainly to your advantage if electrical and water supplies are incorporated. The structure must be entirely finished before any birds are even purchased.

SITE

Depending on the space available, you may have little choice in the actual site. Do attempt to choose a spot within view of your home. Avoid siting aviaries directly under trees. Such a situation has the following disadvantages: the ground can be damp; fallen leaves in the autumn add to the dampness, and the time spent removing the leaves from the aviary roof is better expended on other jobs in the aviary. Furthermore, overhanging branches attract cats and birds of prey. The presence of these predators is stressful to conures. Rodents use the branches to gain access to the flight roof. Perching wild birds will drop their feces into the flight. Certain trees exude toxic substances from the foliage, branches and buds. Lastly, the tree may screen the flight from the benefits of sunshine.

Thick-billed Parrot, *Rhynchopsitta pachyrhyncha.* Many experts believe that parrots kept in outdoor aviaries are hardier and more resistant to disease than indoor birds.

A wall or screen of bushes on one or two sides of the aviary provides a good windbreak. A pleasant backdrop is also afforded. If possible, have the flight facing the south or east (in the northern hemisphere) so that it receives the benefit of the early morning sunshine. It is also protected by its shelter from cold northerly or westerly winds. Try not to site the aviary on the lowest part of your property; this is obviously the wettest area.

AVIARY BASE

Basically there are four choices for the aviary base: bare earth, gravel, concrete and slabs.

Bare earth

Dirt is already on site, so it costs nothing. Birds enjoy pecking over this, but this is its only advantage. Bare earth becomes unsightly with the passing weeks. It is also the least hygienic. It looks like a mud bath during bad weather. The earth should be covered with a strong welded wire to prevent the burrowing of mice or rats.

Gravel

Laid to a depth of about 15 cm (6 in), gravel prevents most weeds from growing through. It is easily hosed with water and raked to keep it clear of feces. It is available in various sizes and colors. Gravel placed on the site looks neat and tidy. The birds will enjoy pecking over it for mineral grit and insects. The gravel is best placed over a screen of weld wire or a layer of concrete to discourage burrowing rodents. Since gravel is difficult to walk on, strategically place a few stepping stones or add a paved pathway to the flight.

Concrete

A few inches of concrete prevents rodents and foxes from burrowing under the flight. It is also very easy to keep clean with regular hosing down. Incorporating a slight slope away from the shelter helps to run-off rainwater. Cover an escape hole for this at the end of the flight with a fine gauge welded wire. It is best if the concrete extends beyond the aviary perimeter to form a walk around the aviary and shelter. A coloring agent (perhaps a green or greenish brown) can be added to the concrete to take away the

better. Length is particularly important as conures are very strong flying birds. Great size is not vital to breeding conures, but the object of keeping these beautiful birds is to have the pleasure of seeing them enjoy themselves. If you initially set a high standard for your aviaries, then anything smaller will be unacceptable to you. Packing as many conures into as small a space as possible should be disagreeable to anyone.

Breeding conures must be housed in individual pairs. Serious fighting will ensue otherwise. The reason fighting occurs is not because the birds are unduly aggressive to their own kind, it is because few aviculturists devote the amount of space needed to keep more than one pair in harmony.

A person intending to breed a few pairs of conures will probably opt for a row of aviaries. Each should have flight lengths of about 3 m (10 ft) with widths around 1 m (3 ft). The height is best over 2 m (6.5 ft). This makes viewing the aviary better; your vision is not distracted by the roofline.

bare look. The only drawbacks to concrete bases are that they take a while to lay down and, once down, are rather permanent.

Slabs

Slabbing is a quick, attractive and flexible option for an aviary base. It is also the most expensive option. Paving slabs are the least costly, while color coated slabs are the most expensive. Attractive designs can be made within the aviary by using just a few colored slabs. These days all sizes are available. You can work out the sizes needed for a neat fit at the edges. The slabs are best laid on a base of sand and small gravel chips.

AVIARY SIZE

The larger the aviary, the

AVIARY DESIGN

The most popular shape for an aviary is rectangular. Round and octagonal shapes can be built as well. These latter shapes may be more attractive, though more expensive to build. They may also be less convenient to service than those in a straight row of flights.

If you have a row of aviaries, even if only two or three, then a useful idea is to have a wired-in corridor at the end of the flights. This serves two purposes. First, it acts as a safety porch. Should any conures manage to fly past you as the aviary door is open, they will be trapped in the safety porch. Second, if a large aviary is built at the end of the corridor, this can be used as a stock flight for young or non-breeding birds. The advantage of such a design is that the birds do not need to physically be caught to be transferred from the aviary to the stock cage. They can simply be ushered from one to the other by opening their aviary door at the end of the corridor.

If you have an aviary that is 2 m (6.5 ft) wide, this can be built so that a divider can be attached as required to convert it into two individual sections. A similar division can be added to the shelter. Aviaries can be built with extra storage space to store food and equipment.

FLIGHT MATERIALS

The flight should be constructed using weld wire rather than chicken wire. Chicken wire quickly loses its shape and is not strong enough to contain these powerful birds. The minimum wire gauge that should be used is 19. A lower number is even better, though more costly. The gauge refers to the thickness of the wire. The hole size is ideally 1.25 cm x .62 cm (.5 x .25 in) to prevent vermin from entering. Most breeders use a larger size, say 2.5 cm x 1.25 cm (1 x .5 in). They place a finer mesh around the bottom 62 cm (2 ft) of the aviary with the top curling away from the flight.The framework should be of stout timber not less than 5 x 5 cm (2 x 2 in) thick. Cover the inner frame edges with aluminum strips or fine mesh to protect against the gnawing of the conures. Double wire adjacent flights to prevent the conures from biting the

feet of their neighbors.

It is best if the aviary is constructed of frames of suitable size and these are simply bolted together. Such aviaries are readily dismantled, extended or moved. The frames can be mounted on a small brick or wooden wall for added attraction. The wood can be treated with a preservative. This also gives some added color.

As an alternative to wood, and much longer lasting, use angular or tubular metal alloys. These can be cut and shaped by most small engineering companies or even at your local garage.

However, this is probably more costly.

Along the part of the roof near the shelter, furnish a solid or Plexiglas cover. The birds can sit in the aviary, yet be out of the rain. Likewise, sheeting can be placed along part of the flight near the shelter to protect the birds from cold wind. These side covers can be removed during the warmer months.

Food stations should be placed under cover towards the back. An inspection hole can be made in the back wall of the aviary. This way the food and water pots can be refilled without entering the flight.

INDOOR ACCOMMODATIONS

A shelter within a birdroom must contain a pop-hole. Through this the conures can exit from the shelter into the flight. It is handy if this pop-hole has a control by which the birds can be shut up in the shelter. This is easily arranged by having a drop-down door to the pop-hole, which is raised or lowered with a wire wrapped around a pulley outside the aviary. A landing platform or perch should be fitted below the hole.

The internal shelter may be full headroom size, or it may be raised from the floor to provide storage room below. This can be the feeding station as well as an alternative roosting site for the birds. The raised shelter can have a base of welded-wire so that seed husks and feces can fall through. They enter a funnel-type slope and are deposited into a trash bin.

The shelter needs to contain only a couple of sturdy perches. If the shelter is of the floor-to-ceiling type, ensure that the floor has a good covering that can be easily cleaned—for instance, thermoplastic tiles or linoleum.

The remainder of the birdroom should have as much shelf and working space as possible. It is amazing just how much extra equipment, cages, food and other items you will acquire. The walls of a wooden birdroom should be lined to help maintain a more stable temperature. Of course, no wiring should be within reach of the conures. It is best to hide all wiring behind the wall or encase it in metal tubes.

INDOOR FLIGHTS

The indoor flight should be as large as space permits. Conures will happily breed in such an accommodation. In order to save flight space, it is better to fit nest boxes outside the flight. Cut the cage wires to give the birds access to the nest box. Considering the conures' whittling tendencies, it is also worthwhile to cover the outside of the nestbox with welded-wire.

Resist the temptation to overcrowd the birdroom with indoor flights and breeding cages. Not only do you increase the health risk factor but you reduce the amount of free space in the aviary.

Cover the windows in an internal flight with mesh. This prevents the conures from bashing themselves against the clear glass. Additionally, the windows can be opened on warm days without fear of any birds escaping.

An extra room or an unused garage or shed can be used as an internal flight. Such buildings can make fine accommodations. Incorporating extra windows ensures that plenty of sunshine can enter. Remember to fit a safety porch so that there is no risk of the birds escaping as you enter.

An internal flight can be constructed in your home if your conures are kept purely as pets. Such a flight is far superior to a mere cage. It could be built into an alcove or spare room. The frame can be stained and decorated to be esthetically pleasing.

Bear in mind that when preparing any accommodation for conures,

it must be draft-free. Birds can cope with colder weather, but not with drafts. Likewise, birds should never be housed in a manner that prevents them from escaping the rays of the sun. A shaded spot must always be available.

CAGES

There is a wide variety of cages marketed by pet shops, many of which are excellent. Some are flimsy in construction and poorly designed. Choose a strong cage made to house large birds. Essentially, a simple box shape is the most practical cage for any bird.

Select one that is sturdy in construction. It should be large enough for the conure to extend its wings fully. There should be plenty of space below the perches for the tail and space above for the head. Fit two perches at different heights so that the bird can clamber from one to the other. Many cages come with only two feeding dishes, but four dishes are desirable. The cage door should have an "anti-conure" latch. These birds are very intelligent and can learn how to open simple latches quickly.

Typical cage for one of the smaller species of conures. Length and width should be very important considerations when purchasing a cage.

Some cage models have pull-out tray floors to facilitate cleaning. Others are made so that the base can be unclipped from the cage wires for cleaning purposes. Again, a nice extra in a cage is a grating just above the cage floor so that seed and feces do not accumulate on the cage floor and the bird is kept away from the mess.

Stands for parrot cages should be solid. There should be no risk of the cage getting knocked over. A small table is actually very good for this purpose.

EQUIPMENT

Perches are the main requirement for either an aviary or cage. Wooden dowels of varying thickness exercise a bird's feet. Generally, diameters between 1.25 cm and 5 cm (.5–2 in) are well suited to conures. Natural branches of fruit trees make ideal perches. Be sure that they are from trees or bushes which are free of chemical sprays, pesticides, etc. A conure will enjoy nibbling at the leaves, buds, and bark. This chewing is good for the birds. It provides amusement and nutrition.

Such branches, of course, need replacing on a regular basis.

Food and water containers are best made of earthenware or aluminum. These can be washed easily and are less likely to be destroyed like those made of plastic. Feed containers must always be placed under cover in aviaries to prevent contamination from droppings. Do not place them directly below any perches.

Bird nets are a useful aid

Many birds enjoy sitting outside their cage; some, however, will only sit on top of it. A landing perch is designed to attach to the top of your bird's cage to make the time it spends there more comfortable. Your local pet store carries such items. Photo courtesy of Rolf C. Hagen Corp.

in an aviary to secure a conure quickly. These are readily available from your local pet shop in varying sizes. Purchase one with a diameter of about 30 cm (12 in). If possible, have both a long- and short-handled one, or one with interchangeable handles.

Ionizers have become very popular with birdkeepers. The more birds you have in an enclosed space, the more desirable this plug-in accessory becomes. An ionizer releases millions of negative ions. They attach themselves to airborne dirt and bacteria, and make them fall to the ground. Here they are gathered with other debris when you clean. The number of units needed is determined by the size of your birdroom. They are economical to run—a real boon to hygiene. They are also reasonably priced.

Heaters may be more of a benefit to you than to the birds. Conures can often cope with cold weather. Special units which can be thermostatically controlled are now adapted for bird breeders. Choose a model that will heat to the required level, yet not create a furnace! The heater must only keep the air from becoming chilly; high-powered models are rarely needed. Alternatively,

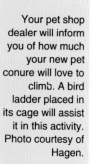

Your pet shop dealer will inform you of how much your new pet conure will love to climb. A bird ladder placed in its cage will assist it in this activity. Photo courtesy of Hagen.

All birds enjoy a swing in their cage. Conures are no exception to this. There are many styles and sizes available at your local pet shop to choose from. Photo courtesy of Hagen.

electric tubular heaters, as used in horticulture, are best. Avoid any gasoline or butane-based heaters.

The latest heaters also double as cooling fan units. Check them out if your finances allow. If you have no cooling system, fill two or three buckets with water. Cover them with mesh. These won't really cool the birdroom although they will create the needed humidity during warm periods if your birds are breeding indoors.

Lighting is best if wired to a timer switch. Ideally, it should also have a dimmer so that the birds are not plunged into sudden darkness. A low-watt blue nightlight can be a lifesaver. It can save a bird from dying as a result of night fright.

EXTRAS

Among the many items available today are automatic seed dispensers, platforms and hospital cages. Investment in extra equipment is not essential to good results in birdkeeping. However, it certainly makes things easier. Most important in good husbandry is the effort you put into taking care of your birds.

Feeding

Most parrot species, conures included, are quite adaptable in their feeding habits. Often this has proven vital to their survival. For example, for a number of years parrots from the neotropics were given diets based on that of the Australian parrots. These Australian birds exist in the arid regions of that continent. They subsist on little else than seeding grasses. It was assumed that most other parrot species would also subsist on such a diet. The truth is that African, Asiatic and South American parrots have access to a vast range of fruits, leaf buds, nuts and vegetables.

Eventually breeders realized that parrots from other continents needed more varied diets. Consequently there was a dramatic increase in the number of species that would breed in captivity. This does not mean that your conures will automatically accept a varied diet. Birds are creatures of habit. If they are not used to variety, they may refuse beneficial foods simply because they are unfamiliar.

Likewise, recently imported birds may have received only a basic ration since their capture. Their feeding habits can be modified repeatedly, offering a good variety on a regular basis.

Apart from their quieter disposition, the Dusky-headed Conure, *Aratinga weddellii,* can be recommended for their good behavior in not chewing every bit of woodwork in sight.

FEEDING UTENSILS

The owner of one or two pet conures needs little more in the way of utensils than those provided with the cage. Usually extra seed containers are required. This way seeds may be offered separately rather than as a mixture because birds tend to discard those seeds not especially liked when all mixed together. Birds eat their favorite items first. Only when these are gone will the next preferred item be eaten. Also, if all the seeds are in one container, the smaller ones tend to fall to the bottom of the feeder.

Uncovered, hook-on-type feeders can be replaced by feed hoppers with plastic viewing panels. These feeders hold more seed, are self-dispensing and the seed levels can be more easily observed. There is another benefit. Once eaten, the seed husks are dropped aside by the conure. Having a covered seed dish prevents the husks from falling on top of the uneaten seed. Sometimes a bird cannot find the fresh seed underneath the husks, or you may think the dish is filled with seed when in fact it is full of husks! Periodically tap self-dispensing feeders to check that the seeds are falling into the trays. Occasionally

All birds enjoy Spray millet as an addition to their regular diet. This can be purchased at your local pet shop in various quantities. Photo courtesy of Hagen.

33

a chute becomes clogged. Those designed for larger parrots are typically wider. Some have adjustable openings to accommodate the larger seeds.

Water may be given via open containers or gravity water bottles. If using bottles, purchase those with metal tips. Plastic tips are soon destroyed. The best water dish is probably an earthenware crock. A conure also can bathe by splashing the water over itself if the dish is large enough. This dousing is excellent for feather condition.

Grit and cuttlefish bone are two other essentials. Grit aids in digestion. It is best given in its own small container. A clip can be purchased to hold a cuttlefish bone to the cage bars. Cuttlefish bone provides calcium. Gnawing on the bone also helps to keep the beak in condition.

The breeder with many birds will find the large chicken-type seed containers handy. This greatly reduces the time spent refilling seed pots. Feed dishes must still be checked routinely on a daily basis, though. Any sudden drop in the amount eaten is the first sign that a bird may be ill.

Breeders require numerous items. These include buckets, plastic tubs and other containers. Stored in these are chopped fruits, vegetables and sprouted seeds prepared in bulk and placed in a refrigerator. Seed must be kept fresh, clean and dry at all times. Do not store more than a month's supply of seed as the risk of spoiling increases.

By all means, shop around for good value. Remember, though, that cheap seed is usually less clean and of less nutritional value. Do not compromise low cost for quality. This is false economy.

Wash all greenfoods before offering them to your conures. Many have been treated with harmful pesticide chemicals. Local plants and grasses can be gathered and offered to your birds. However, avoid collecting wild plants from roadsides which have likely been contaminated by motor fumes. Also avoid areas fouled by other animals.

ROUTINE

Feed your birds at the same time each day. Early

morning and late afternoon are good as fresh foods will not sour as quickly as when they are given during the hottest part of the day. The conures soon become used to a routine. Of course, seed and water must be available 24 hours a day. Planning and feeding a varied weekly menu for your birds assures that you will not omit any useful items from the diet.

No food should be given suddenly in large quantities. Conures must be acclimated to dietary changes. All greenfoods should be fed in regular quantities to prevent illness.

Three different varieties of how millet grows in the wild. Clipping it to the side of an aviary in this fashion is the best way to offer it to your birds.

DIETARY CONSTITUENTS

A whole range of foods that ensure your birds have a wholesome and well-balanced diet exists. Rarely can the same foods be offered as the conures obtain in the wild. Fortunately, foods with the same constituent values can be supplied.

SEEDS

Seeds can be divided into two broad groups based on their content: those rich in carbohydrates and those containing large amounts of protein and fatty oils.

Carbohydrates are the compounds that provide your birds with energy for daily activities, such as flying, climbing and similar muscular activities. Activity also creates heat. Hence, an active bird is less likely to suffer the effects of chilling than a bird with no regular exercise.

Seeds rich in carbohydrates are: wheat, white millet, yellow millet, maize, and canary seed.

These seeds also contain proteins and fats. The amount is comparatively small. Canary seed and millet are the most common given to conures. They also provide much occupational therapy to your conures. Since these seeds are small, it takes the birds quite a time to shell and consume a quantity. Millet is also available as sprays on stalks. These are well liked by almost all birds. The spray can be hung up as a bunch in the cage or aviary.

Carbohydrate seeds may be regarded as the basic ration of your bird's diet. They are needed throughout the year. Other seeds are given on a more controlled basis.

Protein and fat-rich seeds provide conures with the basic building materials for building tissue. They are essential for growing chicks. The fatty oil helps in the absorption and production of vitamins, as well as in the general metabolic processes of the body.

Any excess proteins and fats are stored in the body. They provide a layer of subcutaneous insulation to provide warmth. However, this layer must not be too thick, otherwise the bird is overweight. Obesity is an unhealthy condition, which affects breeding ability and egg production.

When there are

insufficient carbohydrates in the diet, stored fat is converted into energy. This process continues either until carbohydrates are provided or until the bird has no more fat to convert.

It can be appreciated that protein-rich seeds must reflect the amount of activity of a bird. The more active individual needs more of these seeds than does a sluggard. Breeding pairs need extra protein seeds to meet the increased demands on their bodies. They must have sufficient nutrition to sustain themselves and to pass good health onto their progeny.

When housed correctly and fed a varied diet, the Sun Conure, *Aratinga solstitialis*, proves to be the most prolific member of the genus *Aratinga*.

Protein and fat-rich seeds include the following: pine nuts, peanuts, sunflower, poppy, linseed, rape, hemp and niger. The first three are popular choices with parrot owners. The others, all small seeds, are given in lesser quantities according to individual tastes. Some are ignored altogether. Each of these protein-rich seeds contain small quantities of carbohydrates, ranging from 11–21% and are typically available from pet shops. They are but a small selection of those your birds might enjoy. Varieties such as sesame, safflower and those of most wild grasses offer varying ratios of carbohydrates and proteins.

Conures enjoy many nuts, such as brazils, almonds, hazel nuts, and walnuts. These can be costly if you have more than a few birds. Some smaller species of conures will not be able to crack the shells, and you will need to do it for them.

Many wild plants, such as rose hips, and the berries of shrubs are welcome additions to a bird's diet. If you are unsure of which local vegetation is suitable for your birds, the rule of thumb is, if in doubt, leave it out. Whatever wild birds eat should be safe for your conures.

Beyond carbohydrates and proteins in their natural seed state, these compounds are available in prepared food forms found in pet shops. Dog kibble and breakfast cereals are all forms of carbohydrates. These can be given to your birds mixed with a fruit salad or on their own.

Milk, cheese, fish and chicken are excellent forms of animal protein. They provide certain amino acids not available from plant tissues. Milk-soaked bread is especially good for conures with chicks in the nest, and cheese cut into cubes is always a welcome treat.

Particularly during the breeding season, conures will eat mealworms and other invertebrates. Clean these meals before offering them to the birds. Place them in clean sawdust for a few hours so that they void waste products. Never feed

During the breeding season your birds will require some sort of calcium supplement. Cuttlefish bone and tonic blocks will supply these requirements. Photo courtesy of Hagen.

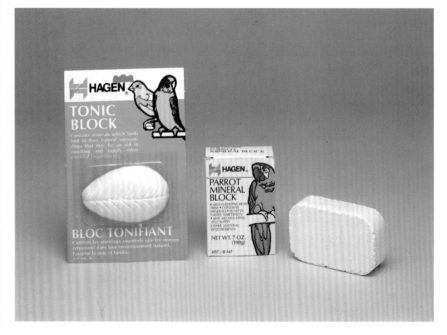

birds fishing bait treated with dye. This may be toxic.

Another form of protein for breeding pairs is insectivorous foods prepared for canaries or soft-billed birds. It is available in pet shops. Prepare this according to the manufacturer's instructions. It can be fed as is or mixed with a fruit salad.

FRUITS AND VEGETABLES

Conures are partial to many fruits and vegetables. These are also an essential part of their diet. They are the richest natural form of vitamins. Birds enjoying a wide variety require no additional vitamin supplements. These foods are largely composed of water (accounting for up to 95% of their weight). They also provide small amounts of carbohydrates, proteins and essential minerals.

The selection of fruits available is extensive: apples, oranges, bananas, melons, pineapples, grapes, pomegranates, plums, peaches, apricots, figs, raisins and dates are just a few. Vegetables include: spinach, celery, beetroot, kale, carrots, brussels sprouts, corn, peas and beans. To this can be added such wild plants as dandelion, shepherd's purse, plantain and chickweed. Once washed, wild plants can be offered complete— roots and all. They can also be chopped and mixed with other foods, or dried, crushed and sprinkled in with seeds.

SOAKED AND SPROUTED SEEDS

Conures enjoy seeds which have been soaked and sprouted. Such seed is especially beneficial during the breeding period. It is also useful to birds recovering from an illness.

Any seeds can be soaked. Simply place a quantity into a bowl of clean, tepid water. Leave them for 24 hours. Rinse them before feeding to the birds. This softened seed is recommended for chicks.

During the sprouting, or germination process, the protein and vitamin content of seed rises dramatically. To sprout seeds after they have been soaked and rinsed, simply place them on a damp paper towel. Leave them in a darkened place for 24–48 hours. Feed the sprouts to the birds when they are just a few millimeters high. Seeds which fail to sprout are not fresh. Only fresh seed should be given to your pets.

VITAMINS AND MINERALS

These compounds are absolutely vital to good health. A deficiency in any one may result in a nutritional imbalance and illness. Likewise, an excess may be equally as damaging.

Vitamins A, E and those of the B group are especially important to parrots. Cod liver oil and wheat germ oil are vitamin rich. Very small amounts can be mixed in with seed.

Of the many minerals needed by birds, the only one you need to supplement continually is calcium. A hen's need for this can rise fourfold during the breeding season. So, apart from

cuttlefish bone, crushed eggshell can be offered in a separate container or mixed in with the grit. Calcium is also available in powder and liquid forms from pet shops.

Grit is essential to all seed-eating birds. It is stored in the gizzard to assist in the breaking down of the seed. (Birds have no teeth to crush seed.) Since grit is composed of numerous minerals, it serves a double role in the digestive process. Grit of a suitable size for conures can be purchased from your local pet dealer.

WATER

Water must always be available to your birds, even if they eat plenty of fruits and vegetables. It should be fresh each day.

Vitamin supplements can be added to your bird's diet either in powder form or liquid. Your local pet shop will carry an assortment from which you can choose. Photo courtesy of Hagen.

Breeding

Breeding conures is a fascinating aspect of the hobby. However, be prepared for setbacks. Having a true pair of birds is merely the starting point. A great deal can go wrong from that point on. Alternatively, watching the first chicks leave the nest is a marvelous moment.

PRE-BREEDING CONSIDERATIONS

Before attempting to breed, a few points must be considered. You must be fully prepared for events as they happen.

Spare cages and aviaries must be on hand. Within weeks, chicks need their own accommodations. Just three breeding pairs might mean up to 15 youngsters. They need housing three months later, maybe less. You do not want to overcrowd your stock. Do not breed too many pairs until you gain experience and have ample

Nanday Conure, *Nandayus nenday.* Since the first importations of this bird, over 100 years ago, the Nanday has remained one of the most instantly recognizable and cheapest members of the conure family.

accommodations for expansion.

Record books are a must. Regardless of how good your memory is, things can be forgotten. Record cards should indicate all pertinent information: which birds were paired and when, how many eggs were laid and how many were fertile, how many chicks were reared, problems, growth, foods, etc. Even matters such as the temperature during breeding can be recorded. Include any information that will create a full history of the birds and the breeding program. Such records might prove invaluable at a later date.

Leg rings are used by many breeders. They are the only proven means of identifying particular birds. Closed metal rings can be placed on chicks when they are a few days old. You must have those of the correct size for the species you keep; an undersized ring can cause the loss of a bird's leg if it becomes too tight. Rings are year-dated and can carry code numbers. This helps ensure that the bird and its records are properly matched.

Hand-feeding utensils are essential in case a hen dies or does not take sufficient care of the chicks. Sometimes supplementary feeding is mandated. Hand-rearing should be done only if required; allow the parents to raise the chicks when possible.

A few items should be readily available if hand-feeding is necessary. A dropper-type feeder is useful. Additionally, a nursery cage is needed. A small aquarium tank can be used. An under floor heater pad for aquariums maintains a constant temperature in the brooder. Of course, brooders can be purchased in a pet shop. A reliable thermometer and thermostat are needed to control the temperature.

BREEDING CONDITION

The birds themselves must be primed for breeding. Only the most fit conures should be expected to breed. The hen should not be carrying too much weight; this could lead to egg-laying problems. An unfit cock may not be able to fertilize the eggs. These facts mean that a breeding pair must be conditioned months before mating even commences. The pair should be getting plenty of exercise. As the season nears, offer extra protein foods.

NEST BOXES

Place nest boxes in the flight prior to introducing the pair. Situate at least two boxes at differing heights in secluded areas. Conures do not like strong sunlight to reach the nestbox.

A popular choice for a nest box is similar to those used for budgerigars and cockatiels, but larger to accommodate the larger size of conures. Overall dimensions of 30 x 30 x 38 cm high (12 x 12 x 15 in) are reasonable. The box should have a hole of a snug fit for the birds to enter. This allows them to fashion the hole to their desired size. This activity also encourages breeding. The hole should be positioned towards the top of the box and to one side, rather than centered. A perch can be placed below the hole, both inside and

Green-cheeked Conure, *Pyrrhura molinae.* This species tends to become very secretive when it begins to lay its eggs. This is caused primarily by the shyness shown in most birds of this species.

outside of the box, to facilitate exits and entrances.

Conures do not need nesting material. A layer of peat or non-chemically treated wood shavings helps to keep the eggs from rolling. A wooden concave block likewise prevents the eggs from being scattered.

The nest box should be made of substantial timber. The conures otherwise will soon chew a hole in the sides or base. A lining of wire mesh inhibits gnawing.

An inspection lid, placed high at the back, should be a built-in feature. The more simple the box is, the easier it is to inspect and clean.

COMPATIBILITY

The next step is to introduce the pair. Usually the pair shows an obvious interest in one another, though not always. If one of the pair attacks the other, separate them. Place them in adjoining cages or aviaries so they are exposed to each other.

Another attempt at putting them together may work. Place them in an aviary or cage unfamiliar to both parties. If this fails, find an alternative mate for one of the pair.

MATING

Some conures mate on a perch; others do so in the privacy of their nest box.

NUMBER OF EGGS

A pair of conures may lay one egg, or as many as eight. Three to five is average for most species. Make a habit of inspecting the nest box on a regular basis. The birds become accustomed to this and will not resent the intrusion. However, make inspections quickly. Talk or hum as you approach the nest box so the birds are aware of your approach. The pair should never be startled. If you own nervous birds, it may be wise to inspect nest boxes as infrequently as possible.

INCUBATION

The eggs are laid on alternate days—one egg every other day. Incubation may commence after the first egg, but more commonly after the third. Typically it is the hen who does all of the incubating. It is not uncommon for the cock to take over the full duties of the female. Generally, the cock simply joins the hen at night. Some males spend short periods during the day with the hen, then roost on the nest box roof or the perch outside the box. The period of incubation is about 26 days. This can vary within a day or two either way. Expect an extra day in cooler weather.

THE CHICKS

Baby conures are born quite helpless. They are covered in a soft grayish down, which gives way to feather quills about the 14th day. The eyes open at about this time. When first hatched, the chicks have no pigment; they are pink in color. The beak and legs show pigment about the 12th day. Growth is rapid and the chicks fledge any time after seven weeks.

If your birds are nervous when you inspect their nest box, weigh the chicks while the parents are out of the box. A lack of a steady increase in a chick's daily

Any bird that has been handled from a very early age will make an extremely trusting and loving pet, whether it's a conure or one of the other parrot species, such as the Hawk-headed Parrots shown here.

weight may indicate that it is not getting its full portion of food. You may have to supply a supplementary feeding to help the chick catch up with its nestmates. Also, recording weights gives you a good idea of the weights to expect of future clutches.

Once the chicks are a few weeks old, the parents have an urge to produce another round of eggs. They may attack the young chicks. If this happens, take the chicks away for hand-rearing. Separate the parents also. A pair should be allowed to raise only one clutch per year. Overbreeding is not healthy for the adults or their progeny.

BREEDING PROBLEMS

A hen not fully fit may have difficulty passing an egg. If she looks distressed and her breathing is labored, place her in a hospital cage immediately. The temperature should be constant around 33°C (91°F). The warmth should result in the lodged egg being laid. If not, get her to a vet quickly or she may die.

Once the egg has been laid, the hen must be reacclimated to the outside temperature. This takes two or three days. If the cock has not taken over incubation of the other eggs, place them in an incubator or under another hen at the same stage of development. Do not overburden another conure if she already has a good-sized clutch.

It is normal for one or more eggs not to hatch. A number of reasons can be cited. Sometimes a minor crack allows bacteria into the egg, and the embryo is killed. The egg may have been very thick or double shelled, and the chick was unable to break out, and died in the shell. The embryo may have been deformed, or the egg may have been chilled if the parents left the nest box for too long. If all of the eggs failed to hatch, the chances are that they were not fertilized.

Another occasional problem is that a hen might start picking the feathers of the chicks. Should this occur, remove the chicks, and do not breed the hen in the future because such a habit is likely to reoccur.

Jandaya Conure, *Aratinga jandaya.* Hatching birds in incubators is a difficult task. One must be sure the eggs are turned daily and that the proper levels of humidity and temperature are kept constant.

HAND-REARING

Hand-rearing is an extremely time-consuming occupation. The younger the chicks, the more time needed. The chicks must be fed every few hours around the clock.

A small spoon or an eyedropper is a useful feeder. Take great care not to pump food into the chick's windpipe. Gauge when the chick has had sufficient food by watching its crop fill up. Chicks are greedy. They will still beg for food when they are full! After feeding, wipe the beaks clean. Dried food causes sores.

Hand-fed birds should be kept in a brooder. Have the heating element at one end so the chicks can move in and out of the warmth at will. If the chicks show any signs of panting, reduce the temperature by a few degrees. Unfeathered chicks are content at a heat level around 32°C (90°F).

Offer hand-fed chicks thicker food as they grow. Place some soaked seed in the brooder. Weaning is a gradual process. It requires a lot of patience.

Hand-fed conures make fantastic pets. They have no fear of handling. Bear in mind, though, that even these birds may be aggressive towards humans when raising their own chicks.

Do not breed conures less than 18 months old. Birds younger than this are more likely to encounter problems. The chicks they produce may be less vigorous.

The Pet Conure

Conures of any age can make delightful pets. Older birds require more time to be tamed. Conures acquired as young birds and given plenty of attention are quieter than older birds.You may be given a basic instruction sheet when you purchase your conure, this should explain what the bird has been eating and any other relevant information. It is important to know this information about your particular bird, not just conures in general.

White-eyed Conure, *Aratinga leucophthalmus*. Whichever species attracts one's initial attention, keeping parrots of any type can become very addictive. A single acquisition is unlikely to remain that way for long!

Put the bird into its new cage once home. The cage should be on a firm table base and out of drafts. If the cage is near a window, be sure it is partly shaded during the day so your pet can move out of direct sunlight.

PLAYFORMS

Being intelligent animals, parrots need plenty of things to occupy their time. Mirrors, bells, and chew toys are lots of fun. A combination playform-feeding station can be purchased. This is a platform of ladders, a climbing frame and maybe a swing. Feeder pots should be at the outer edges. A playform may be a small unit standing on a table, or it can be a much larger construction accommodating a number of birds.

The advantage of such a play area is that a bird soon knows that it is its own. The conure can chew and climb without being reprimanded. It quickly flies to the playform to see if any new items have been added.

"Toys Birds Really Play With"

ACTIVE

An assorted variety of Active Bird Toys can be found on display at your local pet shop. Brightly colored and gnawable, toys prove to make the time your bird spends within its cage fun and exciting.

WING CLIPPING

Some owners always keep their pet's wings clipped. Others only do so initially, yet others never at all. Clipped wings re-grow at the next molt. After the initial clip, the conure needs its wings trimmed every year if you want to keep them in that condition. Feathers properly trimmed are discernible only when the conure extends its wings. Wing clipping should never leave a bird unsightly.

The amount of clipping determines the extent of flying capability. All birds should be able to flutter a short distance and in a straight line. If only one wing is trimmed, a bird cannot control its flight direction. Ultimately, such birds make no attempts to fly. Initially, have your vet or pet shop dealer clip the bird. An experienced handler can show you the different methods of clipping in order to restrict flight to a given level.

The reason clipping is done is so that a bird cannot escape if a door or window is open. Also, a bird with clipped wings is easier to hand-tame. When the bird flutters to the ground, it more readily steps onto a hand to be lifted. Clipped birds are easier to retrieve; they can fly only a short distance before having to land. Of course, if the wings are trimmed, your pet cannot escape cats or dogs.

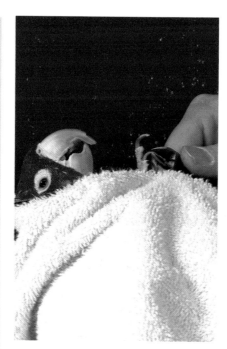

Never leave it unattended when it is out of its cage.

Even a clipped bird becomes a friendly pet only if much time is spent with it. Play with the conure and give it plenty of praise. Never make sudden movements. Always let your pet see what you are doing so it is not startled.

SECURITY

Any caged bird should be allowed out of its cage for exercise. Birds were not meant to live a life of confinement. When your pet is loose, it will want to explore the room. Consider what items are valuable, easily broken and/or chewable. Remove them to make the area bird-proof.

Never let your conure into the kitchen. This room has too many potential hazards. Likewise, electric wires must be kept beyond a conure's reach! Open fires should have guards on them and fish tanks should have canopies.

Never leave your pet unattended with dogs or cats—even if they are well trained. They might hurt the bird in a moment of excitement, even if accidentally. Teach young children how to handle the conure properly. Not only may the conure be hurt, but the child risks a very nasty bite.

BATHING

In the wild, conures bathe in the rain to keep their plumage in healthy condition. Feathers quickly dry out in a centrally heated home. Regular access to baths keeps the feathers moist. The bath can be a shallow bowl of tepid water. The conure will happily splash about. Or, the conure can be sprayed with a fine mist of warm water. Your pet will really enjoy these. It will open its wings and maybe even hang upside down in its cage or on its playform to wet every part of its body. After bathing, place the conure in a warm spot free of drafts. It should be fully dry before nightfall.

SOCIABILITY

If brought up together, conures will live happily with their own species and other similar sized parrots. Caution must be exercised when introducing a new parrot to an established home. The newcomers may be resented to the point of being attacked. Apply common sense as you would with other pets.

Conures are variable in their attitude to family members and visitors. Some may prefer females, while others are happier with males. Some birds accept strangers; others shy away from them. Each conure has its own individual traits. All respond to kindness and gentleness.

TALKING

Conures may learn a few words. They are not high on the list of talking parrots, though. Mere ability to mimic the human voice is a poor reason to own any parrot. They have so much more to offer by way of playfulness, inquisitiveness and companionship.

SCREECHING

Conures have the capacity to make a great deal of noise if so inclined. This tendency can be discouraged in numerous ways, though a bird should not be completely barred from exercising its natural voice.

Certain sounds (such as vacuum cleaners) cause a parrot to screech. Move the

The Jandaya Conure, *Aratinga jandaya,* is not well known for its speaking ability, however, it does prove to be quite a comical pet.

cage to another room when such incidents occur. Sometimes a conure screams simply to gain your attention, or in protest because you have put it back in its cage when it wanted to play. Screeching can be a sign of excitement, well-being, boredom or frustration.

Try to determine why the bird is screeching and remedy the situation. Sometimes placing a cloth over the cage does the trick. Conures are social birds. They are happiest when involved with you.

TEACHING TRICKS

A conure can be taught to do simple tricks. Before this is possible, you must gain the bird's confidence.

A conure can be trained to ring a bell, roll a ball, climb a ladder and spread its wings. Use your imagination to develop tricks. A conure can even be taught to "shake hands." This is easy because parrots often extend a foot when they want to be picked up. Simply hold the foot gently and shake it. Before doing so, say "How do you do?" This eventually triggers the desired response. Reward the conure with lavish praise and a tidbit.

The key to success is repetition and reward. Tricks are mastered with time and patience. Once a conure learns its first trick or two, others are picked up more quickly.

A secret of training is the use of subtle response signals not noticed by observers. These may be phrases or hand movements which become associated with certain maneuvers.

Health

A well-cared-for bird, given a balanced diet, is not likely to have problems. Of course, any bird can become ill or injured. This chapter discusses the more common problems that respond to home treatment. More serious matters must be referred to a veterinarian.

One or two pet conures are less likely to experience health problems than a large flock of birds. Pet birds live in a more controlled environment. They are not exposed to as many potential dangers.

If a bird dies without apparent reason, have your vet perform an autopsy. The cause of death should be established. If possible, remedy the situation to prevent future losses of other birds.

QUARANTINE

All subsequent additions should be subjected to a quarantine of 21 days before being introduced to an established stock. This applies regardless of the quality of the source from which your birds came. A bird may be incubating a disease not yet apparent. Also during this period you can check that the bird is feeding correctly.

HOSPITAL CAGE

Every bird owner, even those with a single pet, should have a hospital cage. These units can be purchased at a pet shop. A hospital cage enables an ill bird to be exposed to a constant raised temperature. Often heat alone cures most common complaints.

You can construct a hospital cage from a box-type cage with a wire front; A wired cage front allows for ventilation. Paint it with a washable paint, or make the hospital cage from substantially coated wood. These are easy to wipe clean. Saving just one bird is worth the cost.

Mount an infrared lamp to the cage front, or suspend it from above. Offset the lamp to the side of the cage. Setting the lamp to the side allows the bird to move closer or further from the heat source as it desires. Cover this with 2.54 x 2.54

cm (1 x 1 in) weld wire. A reliable thermometer is required. A thermostat is useful for adjusting the temperature, which should be about 32–35°C (90–95°F).

There are auxilliary lighting tubes available which produce ultra-violet light. These lamps provide sick birds with the benefit of artificial sunshine.

Do not abruptly remove a bird from a hospital cage. A sudden drop in temperature could be devastating to a recovering bird. Reduce the temperature over a number of days until the normal living level is reached.

ISOLATION

Isolate a conure at the first sign of illness. Delay allows the problem to worsen and to spread to other stock. Consult your vet if the problem seems serious.

If the bird is taken to a vet, it may be useful to collect some feces for microscopic examination. Many ailments can be identified only by such a process.

COMMON COMPLAINTS

The most common minor ailments are colds, diarrhea and parasitic infection. Heat treatment usually cures diarrhea. Sometimes, though, diarrhea is not an illness in itself, but it is a symptom of another, more serious problem. Should diarrhea persist after greenfoods have been withheld for a few days, seek veterinary advice.

Of the parasites typically encountered, red mites, lice and feather mites are the most troublesome. Red mites can be especially bad; they spend only part of their life on their hosts. After

Although not as brightly colored as the other conure species, Hoffman's Conure, *Pyrrhura hoffmanni*, makes a wonderful and confiding pet.

sucking blood, they hide in crevices in the birdroom or cage. Thus cleanliness is vitally important to prevent infestations of these pests. Parasites reduce the vigor of your birds. Other bacteria are introduced via the wounds created, resulting in secondary infections.

Red mites can also attack nest boxes. The chicks are seriously drained of energy; they become anemic. Parents suffer so much discomfort and loss of sleep that they cannot even prompt the chicks to desert the nest.

Red mites can be seen as quick-moving, tiny grayish specks. Eradication of them is possible only by treating the cages and nest boxes, as well as the birds. Both the adult mites and their eggs must be destroyed. Burn the perches and nesting material.

Lice are slow-moving creatures that spend their whole life on their hosts. They spread by moving from one bird to the other when the birds are sitting together. Their eggs cling to the feathers. Commercial sprays and powders kill all lice, mites and similar arachnids.

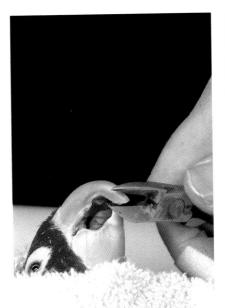

Red-masked Conure, *Aratinga erythrogenys,* having its beak trimmed. This procedure should only be performed by your veterinarian or someone who has much experience.

All birds have worms in their intestinal tracts. This is normal. However, if these reach large numbers, a bird's health can be adversely affected. Worming is a must and is best done prior to the breeding season. Repeat treatment after ten days is required to kill later hatching eggs. Numerous vermifuges are available from pet shops.

It is possible to treat certain complaints by adding solutions to the drinking water. This is an acceptable procedure,

55

although there is no reliable way of determining the dosage ingested by the bird. Oral administration is the preferred method. A dealer or vet can show you how to hold a parrot without getting a nasty nip.

BEAKS AND NAILS

Both beaks and nails may become overgrown. Trim them to a reasonable length using a pair of dog clippers. Be careful not to cut the blood vessel. This is easily seen in pink-colored nails and beaks, but much more difficult to see through black pigment. Trim a little at a time to safeguard against an accident. Use a styptic pencil or talcum powder to arrest minor bleeding.

MOLTING

The molt is a trying time for all birds. The sooner it is accomplished, the better. Birds should have access to regular bathing facilities. This is a great aid to the molting process. In very warm, dry homes, some parrots may be in an almost perpetual molt. This is known as a soft molt. Birds seem to adjust to this without undue problems. Supply birds with vegetables, such as carrots, when they are molting.

A pair of canine nail clippers may be used to clip your birds nails, however caution must be exercised when performing such a task so that the "quick" or blood vessel is not cut.

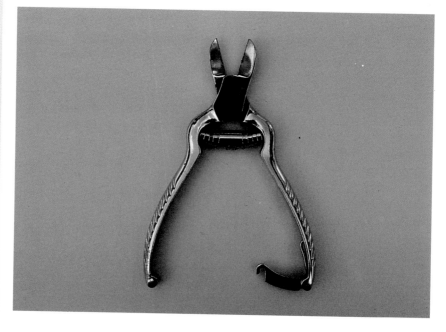

CUTS AND BROKEN LIMBS

Minor cuts usually heal without treatment. A wipe with a mild antiseptic is all that is needed. Serious wounds should be referred to your vet. Wrap the bird in a towel so that it is immobilized. Protect it from abrupt temperature fluctuations and drafts during transport.

Broken wings or limbs are not easy to treat. A bird can be substantially impaired if a limb or wing is not set properly. The wing or limb must be placed back into its correct position. Sometimes splints are made. The problem is keeping them on. A bird can do itself more damage trying to take them off.

Keep the bird in a warm, quiet spot. Remove all perches. Broken limbs mend within a couple of weeks. It may be that the wing or leg is in a slightly different

position. Other than this, the bird should be just fine.

TUMORS AND OTHER GROWTHS

A bird, especially as it gets older, may suffer from tumors or various other growths. These are generally in the area of the chest or throat. Some are benign, others are not. Either way, your vet will advise you of the best course of action.

A conure can be stung by a wasp, or the skin could be pierced by a thorn. Either may result in a growth or local abscess. Clean the infection daily with an antiseptic cream or lotion.

STRESS

A major killer of birds is stress. Indeed, it may be the biggest single cause of death, either directly or secondarily, accompanying an illness. Stress burns up mental and physical energy. A bird quickly loses vigor. It is thus open to attack by bacteria, parasites or other problems. What makes stress difficult to treat is that its cause is not always understood.

The proximity of an aggressive bird to another can cause the other bird

Blue-crowned Conure, *Aratinga acuticaudata*. Bright, clear eyes that show no signs of inflammation or discharge are indications of good health.

stress. Moving a cage or the bird itself from one place to another often creates stress. Generally, captured wild birds are far more likely to be stressed than are homebred birds or young birds. The loss of a breeding mate or a companion can trigger a state of stress.

Be watchful of situations that might give a bird cause for stress. If possible, avoid or remedy the situation.

There are two crucial aspects of keeping birds in good health: good husbandry and familiarizing yourself with the characteristics of your birds. Conures need clean quarters and a proper diet. Any change in their normal behavior might indicate that something is wrong. Reacting promptly and effectively may well make the difference between survival and death.

Brown-throated Conure, *Aratinga pertinax*. Good hygiene practiced daily is the best way to safeguard against disease.

Conure Species

There are approximately 45 parrot species that could be described as conures. These comprise a total of 113 subspecies within nine genera. The genera *Aratinga* and *Pyrrhura* account for about 35 of the species. Although well over half of these have been bred in captivity, they have not been well established. Species formerly imported in large numbers are now rarely seen since export restrictions have been imposed.

Comparatively few conures are available in reasonable numbers. In the case of the more brightly colored species, demand considerably exceeds supply. It is not possible to review each species in this small book. Listed is a representative selection of species usually on sale in

pet shops. Descriptions have been kept to a minimum because most species are basically green birds. The head colors are usually the main features.

As a general rule, birds of the genus *Pyrrhura* are of quieter voice than other conures. These appeal to breeders and pet owners living in more populated areas.

The term "conure" is a general one. There is no scientific difference between the terms conure and parakeet. The use of these names is by tradition rather than by scientific determination.

This chapter deals with the popular and generally available species. Popular in this context is not synonymous with readily available, but rather implies very desirable birds.

Finsch's Conure, *Aratinga finschi,* (bottom), displays less red on its head than the Red-masked Conure, *Aratinga erythrogenys* (top).

POPULAR AND AVAILABLE CONURES

1. Nanday Conure

Nandayus nenday

SIZE: 30.5 cm (12 in)

DISTRIBUTION: Southeastern Bolivia, Paraguay, northern Argentina.

COLOR: The head and beak are black. The chest is blue. The rest of the body is green.

COMMENT: The Nanday is one of the most available and least expensive species. It is an excellent breeder, ideal for beginners. It is rather noisy, though it makes a charming pet. This is a monotypic species—it is the only member of its genus.

2. Orange-fronted or Half-moon Conure

Aratinga canicularis

SIZE: 23 cm (9 in)

DISTRIBUTION: Mexico to western Costa Rica.

COLOR: An orange forehead and a blue crown. The beak is horn-colored. The body is green.

COMMENT: The Orange-fronted has been a popular pet conure in the U.S.A. for many years. The opposite is true in the U.K. In spite of the vast numbers exported, its breeding record is poor. Its price increased in the last few years. This has resulted in greater breeding interest. This conure makes a super pet—it is playful and has a louder voice than its small size suggests.

Very similar to the Half-moon is the Peach-fronted or Golden-crowned Conure, *A. aurea*. The Peach-fronted has a black beak.

3. Blue-crowned Conure

Aratinga acuticaudata

SIZE: 36 cm (14 in)

DISTRIBUTION: Much of central and northern South America, including a few offshore islands.

COLOR: A bluish head, sometimes blue on the chest. Otherwise, this is a green bird. The upper beak

Green Conure, Aratinga holochlora holochlora, nominate form.

Jandaya Conure, Aratinga jandaya.

is horn-colored, the lower is black.

COMMENT: Though not an especially colorful bird, this conure is frequently for sale. A lutino mutation has been recorded. Blue-crowned Conures cost about half as much as Orange-fronted Conures.

4. Brown-throated Conure
Aratinga pertinax
SIZE: 25 cm (10 in)
DISTRIBUTION: Brazil, Venezuela, Surinam, the Guyanas, Colombia and numerous islands of the Lesser Antilles.
COLOR: Brown throat and forehead. The upper beak is horn-colored, the lower is more brown. The body is green.
COMMENT: There are 14 subspecies of this conure. It is regularly for sale at a low price. It is more expensive, though, than the Nanday. It is not bred frequently. The names St. Thomas, Curacao and Caribbean Conure refer

Green Conure sub-species, *Aratinga holochlora rubritorquis*.

to various subspecies.

5. Mitred Conure
Aratinga mitrata
SIZE: 38 cm (15 in)
DISTRIBUTION: Central Peru to northwestern Argentina.
COLOR: The forehead and the eye ring are red. Blotches of red are on the cheeks. The beak is a yellowish horn color. The body is green.
COMMENT: This is one of many conures with red feathers in its head and body. It is a large parrot and can be raucous. Breeding reports are few. A single bird costs about the same as a pair of Nandays. This makes it a good buy for such a large bird.

Somewhat similar, though slightly smaller, is Wagler's Conure, *A. wagleri*. This is less seen in captivity.

6. Dusky-headed or Weddell's Conure
Aratinga weddellii
SIZE: 28 cm (11 in)

Dusky-headed Conure, *Aratinga weddellii*.

DISTRIBUTION: Throughout the Amazon basin.

COLOR: The head is a dusky smoke blue. There are brownish feathers on the crown and neck. Otherwise a green bird with a black beak.

COMMENT: The Dusky-headed Conure has become available in numbers only since the late 1970s. It has proven to be quite good in captivity. Hand-reared babies have the reputation of being superb and quiet pets. A Dusky is a good investment and worth breeding.

7. White-eyed Conure

Aratinga leucophthalmus
SIZE: 33 cm (13 in)

DISTRIBUTION: Northern Argentina, north through Brazil to the Guyanas. Also found in Paraguay, Ecuador, Peru, Uruguay and Colombia.

COLOR: An all green bird. There is some red in the body feathers and on the bend of the wing.

COMMENT: It makes a fine pet. This variety is not yet well established in aviaries. This is probably due to its size and rather plain coloring.

8. Jandaya Conure

Aratinga jandaya

SIZE: 30.5 cm (12 in)
DISTRIBUTION: Northeastern Brazil.

COLOR: The Jandaya (Jenday in the U.K.) is one of three truly magnificent conures. It rivals any parrot in the world for beauty. The body color is yellow. This contrasts superbly with the green of the wings and the black beak.

COMMENT: Unfortunately, this species and the other yellow conures have loud voices. This restricts its suitability as a pet. There is no shortage of customers, however. It has proven to be an excellent bird for those establishing studs.

9. Sun Conure

Aratinga solstitialis
SIZE: 30.5 cm (12 in)
DISTRIBUTION: The Guyanas and northeast Brazil.

COLOR: This is variable. It is basically a mix of yellow and orange merging from one to the other. This coloring extends onto the green wings. The beak is black.

COMMENT: The Sun conure is a reliable breeder. It is well established in breeding aviaries. It makes a super pet if acquired as a youngster.